Awake, O Sleeper!

Dag Heward-Mills

Parchment House

AWAKE, O SLEEPER!

First published 2023 by Parchment House

Find out more about Dag Heward-Mills at:

Healing Jesus Campaign
Email: evangelist@daghewardmills.org
Website: www.daghewardmills.org
Facebook: Dag Heward-Mills
Twitter: @EvangelistDag

ISBN : 978-1-64330-526-4

Contents

1. Those Who Sleep Have No Vision 1

2. Eight Things that Happen When You Sleep 6

3. Inappropriate Sleep 14

4. The Evils that Befall a Sleeper 24

5. How to Wake People Up 29

CHAPTER 1

Those Who Sleep
Have No Vision

And have no fellowship with the unfruitful works of darkness, but rather reprove them.

For it is a shame even to speak of those things which are done of them in secret.

But all things that are reproved are made manifest by the light: for whatsoever doth make manifest is light.

WHEREFORE HE SAITH, AWAKE THOU THAT SLEEPEST, and arise from the dead, and Christ shall give thee light.

See then that ye walk circumspectly, not as fools, but as wise,

Redeeming the time, because the days are evil.

Wherefore be ye not unwise, but understanding what the will of the Lord is.

Ephesians 5:11-17

What It Means to Have No Vision

When you are asleep your eyes are closed. When your eyes are closed the organs which give you vision are covered and closed. You no longer have your sight and your vision. To be asleep, therefore, is to lose your sight and your vision.

1.   Sleeping means you lack a vision for your life.

Where there is no vision, the people perish: but he that keepeth the law, happy is he.

Proverbs 29:18

That is why God says that you must awake from your sleep and your slumber. When you have a vision, you work towards it and make sacrifices for it. Your vision causes you to become what you become.

2.   Sleeping means you lack a spiritual vision for your ministry.

And it shall come to pass in the last days, saith God, I will pour out of my Spirit upon all flesh: and your sons and your daughters shall prophesy, and YOUR YOUNG MEN SHALL SEE VISIONS, and your old men shall dream dreams:

Acts 2:17

Many pastors do not have a vision for their ministries. Many pastors are happy with a small congregation once they can get their daily bread and their monthly salaries. I recently spoke to a man of God who has about thirty thousand people in his church every Sunday.

He said to me, "Some years ago, I came across your book *The Mega Church.*"

He continued, "My wife urged me to read the book over and over and it gave me a vision to have the mega church that I now have."

When I went to Korea, I noticed that the idea of having a large church was everywhere. Every pastor on the church board seemed to have a huge church. The vision and idea and goal of having a mega church came alive in me.

Young men in the ministry are supposed to have visions. Visions to do great things for God! Without a great vision, you will not amount to much in the ministry. Attempt great things for God! Expect great things from God! Without a vision you are asleep!

3. Sleeping means you lack a vision for eternity.

If ye then be risen with Christ, seek those things which are above, where Christ sitteth on the right hand of God. SET YOUR AFFECTION ON THINGS ABOVE, not on things on the earth.

Colossians 3:1-2

4. Sleeping means you lack a vision for your marriage.

And the Lord God said, it is not good that the man should be alone; I will make him AN HELP MEET FOR HIM.

Genesis 2:18

You must have visions and dreams for your marriage. You must not just plan to marry and have children. You must have an aim, a goal and a dream to have a great marriage. You must have a vision of finding help for your life.

a. Your vision for marriage must be to live joyfully and happily with someone.

LIVE JOYFULLY WITH THE WIFE whom thou lovest all the days of the life of thy vanity, which he hath given thee under the sun, all the days of thy vanity: for that is thy portion in this life, and in thy labour which thou takest under the sun.

Ecclesiastes 9:9

b. **Your vision for marriage must be to marry and never to "burn" again.**

"Burning" is a problem of those who are not married. You must have a dream to never burn again. You must have a dream that your husband will never burn again.

> I say therefore to the unmarried and widows, it is good for them if they abide even as I. But if they cannot contain, let them marry: for IT IS BETTER TO MARRY THAN TO BURN.
>
> 1 Corinthians 7:8-9

c. **Your vision for marriage must be to have a better life together.**

> TWO ARE BETTER THAN ONE; because they have a good reward for their labour.
>
> For if they fall, the one will lift up his fellow: but woe to him that is alone when he falleth; for he hath not another to help him up.
>
> Again, if two lie together, then they have heat: but how can one be warm alone? And if one prevail against him, two shall withstand him; and a threefold cord is not quickly broken.
>
> Ecclesiastes 4:9-12

d. **Your vision for marriage must be to have ten times more strength.**

> How should one chase a thousand, and two put ten thousand to flight, except their Rock had sold them, and the Lord had shut them up?
>
> Deuteronomy 32:30

e.   **Your vision for marriage must be to obtain favour with God.**

Whoso findeth a wife findeth a good thing, and obtaineth favour of the Lord.

Proverbs 18:22

CHAPTER 2

Eight Things that Happen When You Sleep

And have no fellowship with the unfruitful works of darkness, but rather reprove them.

For it is a shame even to speak of those things which are done of them in secret.

But all things that are reproved are made manifest by the light: for whatsoever doth make manifest is light.

WHEREFORE HE SAITH, AWAKE THOU THAT SLEEPEST, and arise from the dead, and Christ shall give thee light.

See then that ye walk circumspectly, not as fools, but as wise,

Redeeming the time, because the days are evil.

Wherefore be ye not unwise, but understanding what the will of the Lord is.

Ephesians 5:11-17

Eight Things that Happen When You Sleep

1. When you sleep, you ARE RELAXING.

2. When you sleep, you are COMPLETELY STILL and inactive.

3. When you sleep you have NO KNOWLEDGE of anything around you.

4. When you sleep you are NON-RESPONSIVE and non-reactive.

5. When you sleep you are DEATHLIKE and make no further contribution to anything.

6. When you sleep you LIE DOWN.

7. When you sleep you are COMPLETELY SILENT.

8. When you sleep you pause and TAKE A BREAK from the work of ministry.

1. THOSE WHO ARE ASLEEP ARE RELAXING.

During sleep blood pressure drops, muscles relax, breathing slows down and hormones are released. During sleep, the whole body is relaxed and enjoys restoration, relaxation and peace. During sleep, the brain waves slow down and reach their slowest at a stage during sleep.

When Christians are asleep, they are relaxed when there is no reason to relax. It is high time to wake up and to work for the lord. This is not the time to relax. This is not the time to lower the pressure. This is not the time to breathe slowly. Time is short! Jesus is coming soon! It is time to rise out of sleep.

2. THOSE WHO ARE ASLEEP ARE COMPLETELY STILL AND INACTIVE.

To be asleep is to be completely still and relaxed with your organs of activity and movement at rest. The life of a Christian should be full of movement. There is always movement and change when you walk with the Lord. When you are no longer sleeping, there will be genuine movement in your life.

FOR IN HIM WE LIVE, AND MOVE, and have our being; as certain also of your own poets have said, For we are also his offspring.

Acts 17:28

a. **When you sleep, you will not be drawn to the Father. How can you be drawn to something when you are asleep?** When you are not asleep, there will be movement and the Father will draw you to Himself.

No man can come to me, except the Father which hath sent me draw him: and I will raise him up at the last day.

John 6:44

b. **When you sleep, you will not go deeper into the river of God. How can you go deeper into a river when you are asleep?** Keep moving and keep going deeper into the river of the Holy Spirit.

And when the man that had the line in his hand went forth eastward, he measured a thousand cubits, and he brought me through the waters; the waters were to the ankles. Again he measured a thousand, and brought me through the waters; the waters were to the knees. Again he measured a thousand, and brought me through; the waters were to the loins.

Ezekiel 47:3-4

c. **Jesus was not asleep in the ministry. How could Jesus have accomplished all that He did if He was sleeping?** That was why He was moving around, doing good and healing.

How God anointed Jesus of Nazareth with the Holy Ghost and with power: who went about doing good, and healing all that were oppressed of the devil; for God was with him.

Acts 10:38

d. **Paul was not asleep in the ministry. How could Paul have accomplished all that he did if he was sleeping?** Paul travelled more than anybody in the New Testament.

In journeyings often, in perils of waters, in perils of robbers, in perils by mine own countrymen, in perils by the heathen, in perils in the city, in perils in the wilderness, in perils in the sea, in perils among false brethren;

2 Corinthians 11:26

3. **THOSE WHO ARE ASLEEP HAVE NO KNOWLEDGE OF ANYTHING AROUND THEM.**

To be asleep is to lose awareness and knowledge of your surroundings. Once you are asleep, your knowledge, your wisdom and your understanding are put to rest.

a. When you are asleep in ministry, you lack the Spirit of knowledge.

b. When you are asleep in ministry, you lack the Spirit of wisdom.

c. When you are asleep in ministry, you lack the Spirit of truth.

d. When you are asleep in ministry, you lack the Spirit of understanding.

4. **THOSE WHO ARE ASLEEP ARE NON-RESPONSIVE AND NON-REACTIVE TO DANGER.**

a. **When you are asleep in ministry, you are not aware of the dangers of evil spirits.** This is why thieves come in the night when everyone is asleep. Thieves wait for you to be non-responsive and non-reactive to evil. There are many dangerous things in the ministry. Sleeping ministers are not conscious of impending danger. Sleeping ministers give place to the devil all the time. They are not aware of the evil spirits that are walking around through dry places. They are not aware of evil spirits seeking to enter in and find a place in their lives.

Sleeping Christians open the door wide and welcome demons into their lives. A sleeping minister will welcome a disloyal person to have a place at the highest level. He is unaware of the dangers it poses; and he is unaware of the dangers because he is sleeping.

When the unclean spirit is gone out of a man, he walketh through dry places, seeking rest, and findeth none.

Then he saith, I will return into my house from whence I came out; and when he is come, he findeth it empty, swept, and garnished.

Then goeth he, and taketh with himself seven other spirits more wicked than himself, and they enter in and dwell there: and the last state of that man is worse than the first. Even so shall it be also unto this wicked generation.

Matthew 12:43-45

b. **When you are asleep in ministry, you are not aware of the dangers of the flesh.** This is why thieves come in the night when everyone is asleep. To be asleep is to have a reduced awareness of the dangers from your flesh. Apostle Paul was not asleep in the ministry. He was constantly aware of the dangers of his flesh.

But I keep under my body, and bring it into subjection: lest that by any means, when I have preached to others, I myself should be a castaway.

1 Corinthians 9:27

c. **When you are asleep in ministry, you are not aware of the dangers of evil men and evil women.** There are wicked and unreasonable men who can change the course of your destiny.

Finally, brethren, pray for us, that the word of the Lord may have free course, and be glorified, even as it is with you: And THAT WE MAY BE DELIVERED FROM UNREASONABLE AND WICKED MEN: For all men have not faith.

2 Thessalonians 3:1-2

d. **When you are asleep in ministry, you are not aware of the dangers of evil women.** You must be careful of evil women. Evil women can destroy your life. It is important to be conscious of their presence so that you escape from their wickedness.

To keep thee from the evil woman, from the flattery of the tongue of a strange woman. Lust not after her beauty in thine heart; neither let her take thee with her eyelids. For by means of a whorish woman a man is brought to a piece of bread: and the adulteress will hunt for the precious life.

Proverbs 6:24-26

5. **THOSE WHO ARE ASLEEP ARE DEATHLIKE AND MAKE NO FURTHER CONTRIBUTION TO ANYTHING.**

a. When you are asleep, you are deathlike and make no contributions to the ministry.

b. To be deathlike is to be in a state where you cannot be depended on. Dead people cannot be depended on for anything.

c. Dead people do not fellowship with anyone. To be deathlike is to become someone who does not fellowship.

d. Dead people are not attractive. Most people are scared of dead bodies. To be deathlike is to become spiritually unattractive. Indeed, when you are asleep in ministry, you are no longer attractive.

That I may know him, and the power of his resurrection, and the fellowship of his sufferings, being made conformable unto his death;

Philippians 3:10

6. THOSE WHO ARE ASLEEP ARE LYING DOWN.

a. To be asleep is to lie down in such a way as to reduce the force of your ministry.

b. To be asleep is to reduce the effort being applied. Do not reduce the effort you are applying for the ministry.

c. To be asleep is to slacken. To be asleep is to become less strict about sin.

d. To be asleep is to grow milder and less antagonistic to evil.

e. To be asleep is to put yourself in a position where you cannot work. Sleepers are sleeping! They are not working. People who are sleeping can only engage in rest, relaxation and pleasure.

7. THOSE WHO ARE ASLEEP ARE COMPLETELY SILENT.

Very few people talk in their sleep. To be asleep is to be silent. When you are sleeping in the ministry, you do not preach, you do not teach, you do not counsel anyone, you do not witness to people and you do not share Jesus Christ with anyone. Sleepers do not speak! Sleepers do not preach! Sleepers do not teach!

8. THOSE WHO ARE ASLEEP ARE TAKING A BREAK.

This is not the time to stop working. This is not the time to take a break. This is the time to work even harder. This is not the time to sleep. That is why God is telling us not to sleep. If you take a break now, you will be rejoicing too early.

a. To sleep is to stop all the ministry work you are doing.

b. To sleep is to stop working for God.

c. To sleep is to stop praying.

d. To sleep is to stop reading your Bible.

e. To sleep is to stop witnessing.

f. To sleep is to stop all necessary activities and wait for a while.

King Agag was too quick to think that the trouble was over. He thought he could take a break but the trouble was not truly over. Many Christians are resting when they should not be taking a break.

Then said Samuel, Bring ye hither to me Agag the king of the Amalekites. And Agag came unto him delicately. And Agag said, SURELY THE BITTERNESS OF DEATH IS PAST.

And Samuel said, as thy sword hath made women childless, so shall thy mother be childless among women. And Samuel hewed Agag in pieces before the Lord in Gilgal.

1 Samuel 15:32-33

CHAPTER 3

Inappropriate Sleep

And that, knowing the time, that now IT IS HIGH TIME TO AWAKE OUT OF SLEEP: for now is our salvation nearer than when we believed.

The night is far spent, the day is at hand: let us therefore cast off the works of darkness, and let us put on the armour of light.

Let us walk honestly, as in the day; not in rioting and drunkenness, not in chambering and wantonness, not in strife and envying.

But put ye on the Lord Jesus Christ, and make not provision for the flesh, to fulfil the lusts thereof.

Romans 13:11-14

Inappropriate sleep is sleep that is not fitting and proper. It is important to realise that falling asleep at certain times is inappropriate.

Sleeping too much is also inappropriate sleep. Sleeping when you should be praying is inappropriate sleep. Sleeping when you should be studying is inappropriate sleep.

Please do not misunderstand me. Sleep is necessary for your body to rest. Sleep is important for relaxation and to have a break. Sleep is important to improve your productivity and your performance. When people do not sleep well, they have a greater risk of acquiring heart diseases, stroke and even diabetes.

Poor sleep is associated with a lowered immunity from various diseases. As you can see, sleep is important. Indeed, lions in the wild live for about eight years. However, lions in zoos can live for as long as twenty to thirty years. It is believed that the lions in captivity rest more, sleep more and therefore live longer. They do not have to run around hunting for food. Food is brought to them every day.

I believe that it is important to sleep as much as you can. However, there are times when it is inappropriate to sleep. There are also times when it is inappropriate to sleep for so long.

In this chapter, we want to study biblical warnings about inappropriate sleep.

1.   Inappropriate sleep leads to poverty.

HOW LONG WILT THOU SLEEP, O SLUGGARD? WHEN WILT THOU ARISE OUT OF THY SLEEP?
Yet a little sleep, a little slumber, a little folding of the hands to sleep: So shall thy poverty come as one that travelleth, and thy want as an armed man.

Proverbs 6:9-11

This scripture teaches that poverty will come as a traveller to people who sleep too much. Who is a traveller? A traveller

15

is somebody whom you cannot send away. When people travel from a far country and arrive in your home, you cannot tell them to go away because they do not have anywhere else to sleep. They are forced to stay with you because they are travellers and your home is their destination. Through excess sleep, poverty will descend on you like a traveller whom you cannot send away.

Through sleep, "want will come to you as an armed man." "Want" represents your needs, your desires, your necessities and the essentials of life. An armed man is not someone you can send away easily. He is armed and dangerous. He will do what he wants since he is wielding arms. When he arrives in your house, he will demand his pound of flesh. Is that what you want to happen to you?

Sleeping too much always causes poverty. Laziness is believed to be a major cause of intractable poverty. The scripture is clear. Too much sleep and too much rest will lead to poverty. There are several news articles that show ministers of certain nations sleeping in parliament and at important meetings at which serious decisions were being taken. By the time these ministers woke up the deliberations were over and decisions had been taken. You can only expect poverty to come as an armed man to countries that have ministers of state sleeping at their important meetings.

2.   Inappropriate sleep leads to fruitlessness.

As you pass by the field of a sluggard you can understand why there is so much difficulty. The field is overgrown. The land has not been tended to. The vineyard of such a man will not bear the fruit that it needs to. Too much sleep has allowed it to be overgrown with thorns and nettles. The thorns are killing the vines and preventing it from bearing the fruits it should.

This is not the time to relax. Jesus is coming soon. Your life is finishing before your very eyes. Your lack of fruitfulness in the kingdom is a sign that you rest too much and sleep too much. Fruits are borne by tired people!

I went by the field of the slothful, and by the vineyard of the man void of understanding; and, lo, it was all grown over with thorns, and nettles had covered the face thereof, and the stone wall thereof was broken down.

Then I saw, and considered it well: I looked upon it, and received instruction.

Yet a little sleep, a little slumber, A LITTLE FOLDING OF THE HANDS TO SLEEP: So shall thy poverty come as one that travelleth; and thy want as an armed man.

Proverbs 24:30-34

3. Inappropriate sleep shows that you lack understanding.

When Jonah fell asleep in the ship, it was as though he did not understand that everyone's life was in danger. Everyone was desperate, crying to God for help; but Jonah was asleep.

When you sleep instead of praying, it reveals that you do not understand the dangers you are in spiritually.

It reveals that you do not understand the long and short term plans of the enemy. Arise and shine! This is not the time to sleep! This is the time to pray and to fight back. When your life is in danger you must not sleep. You must arise and pray! It is inappropriate to sleep when souls have to be won.

But the Lord sent out a great wind into the sea, and there was a mighty tempest in the sea, so that the ship was like to be broken.

Then the mariners were afraid, and cried every man unto his god, and cast forth the wares that were in the ship into the sea, to lighten it of them. But Jonah was gone down into the sides of the ship; and he lay, and was fast asleep.

17

So the shipmaster came to him, and said unto him, WHAT MEANEST THOU, O SLEEPER? arise, call upon thy God, if so be that God will think upon us, that we perish not.

Jonah 1:4-6

4. Inappropriate sleep reveals spiritual dullness.

When people sleep at church services, it reveals that they are spiritually dull. The disciples fell asleep on the Mount of Transfiguration. When Peter, James and John were taken up to the Mount of Transfiguration, they fell asleep when exciting things were happening. Moses and Elijah appeared from heaven, speaking with the Lord; but Peter, James and John were fast asleep. They had no idea what was happening. They could not relate with the vision. They were heavy with sleep. When Peter rose out of his sleep, all his remarks were inappropriate and out of context. He wanted to build three houses for spiritual beings who had appeared and departed for heaven.

And it came to pass about an eight days after these sayings, he took Peter and John and James, and went up into a mountain to pray.

And as he prayed, the fashion of his countenance was altered, and his raiment was white and glistering.

And, behold, there talked with him two men, which were Moses and Elias:

Who appeared in glory, and spake of his decease which he should accomplish at Jerusalem.

But Peter and they that were with him WERE HEAVY WITH SLEEP: and when they were awake, they saw his glory, and the two men that stood with him.

And it came to pass, as they departed from him, Peter said unto Jesus, Master, it is good for us to be here: and let us make three tabernacles; one for thee, and one for Moses, and one for Elias: NOT KNOWING WHAT HE SAID.

Luke 9:28-33

The disciples also fell asleep in the Garden of Gethsemane, revealing how spiritually dull they were.

Then cometh Jesus with them unto a place called gethsemane, and saith unto the disciples, sit ye here, while I go and pray yonder.

And he took with him peter and the two sons of zebedee, and began to be sorrowful and very heavy...And he cometh unto the disciples, and findeth them asleep, and saith unto peter, what, could ye not watch with me one hour?

Matthew 26:36-37, 40

How could the disciples sleep on such momentous occasions?

5.   Inappropriate sleep reveals a lack of control.

But I discipline my body and make it my slave, so that, after I have preached to others, I myself will not be disqualified.

1 Corinthians 9:27 (NASB)

To discipline your body is to keep it from inappropriate sleep. Keeping your body under control is to control your sleep. Do not think that keeping your body under subjection just has to do with preventing your flesh from indulging in sexual immorality. Sleeping is a need of the flesh. By the grace of God, you will keep your body under control. It is not easy to discipline the body when it wants to sleep. God will bless you! He will strengthen you as you make your body a slave!

6.   Inappropriate sleep is the thief of prayer.

Then cometh Jesus with them unto a place called Gethsemane, and saith unto the disciples, SIT YE HERE, WHILE I GO AND PRAY YONDER.

And he took with him Peter and the two sons of Zebedee, and began to be sorrowful and very heavy.

Then saith he unto them, My soul is exceeding sorrowful, even unto death: tarry ye here, and watch with me.

And he went a little further, and fell on his face, and prayed, saying, O my Father, if it be possible, let this cup pass from me: nevertheless not as I will, but as thou wilt.

AND HE COMETH UNTO THE DISCIPLES, AND FINDETH THEM ASLEEP, AND SAITH UNTO PETER, WHAT, COULD YE NOT WATCH WITH ME ONE HOUR?

Matthew 26:36-40

Watching and praying is more important than fasting and praying because watching and praying is mentioned more in the Bible. People who watch and pray, pray much more than those who fast and pray.

Watching involves staying up at night to pray. If you learn how to stay awake at night and pray, you will pray many more hours than those who claim to be fasting and praying.

Many people who are fasting do not pray much because they are simply waiting for 6.00pm so that they can end their fast. Once you gain control of your sleep patterns and make yourself able to stay awake at night, you will become a mighty prayer warrior.

David Yonggi Cho once told me that he prayed three to five hours every day for over thirty years. Waking up at night to watch and pray was the secret to his amazing prayer life that gave birth to the largest church in the world. Learn to overcome sleep by going to bed early so that you can rise a great while before day. That was the life of Jesus. He rose up a great while before day and spent a long time praying.

And in the morning, rising up a great while before day, he went out, and departed into a solitary place, and there prayed.

Mark 1:35

7.   Inappropriate sleep renders you defenceless.

It is important to defend yourself against all forms of attack. When you sleep too much, your defences will be down. King Saul was surrounded by sleeping soldiers who were supposed to be protecting him. Saul could have died that day because his guards were sleeping. Perhaps, your life will be saved by a prayer meeting that you attend. Perhaps somebody's life will be saved when you stay up and call on God.

You must have faith in prayer warriors. Prayer warriors must have faith in their jobs. You must believe that your role of praying and interceding for God's servant is actually saving his life. Do not sleep when you should be praying.

So David and Abishai came to the people by night: and, BEHOLD, SAUL LAY SLEEPING WITHIN THE TRENCH, and his spear stuck in the ground at his bolster: but Abner and the people lay round about him.

Then said Abishai to David, God hath delivered thine enemy into thine hand this day: now therefore let me smite him, I pray thee, with the spear even to the earth at once, and I will not smite him the second time.

And David said to Abishai, Destroy him not: for who can stretch forth his hand against the LORD's anointed, and be guiltless?

David said furthermore, As the LORD liveth, the LORD shall smite him; or his day shall come to die; or he shall descend into battle, and perish.

The LORD forbid that I should stretch forth mine hand against the LORD's anointed: but, I pray thee, take thou now the spear that is at his bolster, and the cruse of water, and let us go.

So David took the spear and the cruse of water from Saul's bolster; and they gat them away, and no man saw it, nor knew it, neither awaked: for they were all asleep; because a deep sleep from the LORD was fallen upon them.

1 Samuel 26:7-12

8.   Inappropriate sleep opens you up to evil seeds.

But while men slept, his enemy came and sowed tares among the wheat, and went his way.

Matthew 13:25

While you sleep, the enemy is sowing seeds. Sleep speaks of rest, and relaxation. You must not take your ease when the work is not yet done. The enemy is actively sowing seeds of disloyalty in the church. Satan sows seeds of immorality, seeds of backsliding, seeds of jealousy, seeds of ingratitude and seeds of division.

The reason why evil is planted and grows in our midst is because we are sleeping and relaxing whilst evil is being planted around us. What you allow grows! It grows up around you in a way that overwhelms and corrupts all good things that you are doing.

9.   Inappropriate sleep reveals that you lack virtue.

Who can find a virtuous woman? for her price is far above rubies.

The heart of her husband doth safely trust in her, so that he shall have no need of spoil.

She will do him good and not evil all the days of her life.

She seeketh wool, and flax, and worketh willingly with her hands.

She is like the merchants' ships; she bringeth her food from afar.

SHE RISETH ALSO WHILE IT IS YET NIGHT, AND GIVETH MEAT TO HER HOUSEHOLD, AND A PORTION TO HER MAIDENS.

Proverbs 31:10-15

A virtuous woman is one not given to too much sleep. She rises early and does a lot of background work before the house wakes up.

It is not easy to be a wife. The duties of a wife are overwhelming. A lazy wife is a house wrecker. She is full of excuses, reasons and arguments. She is probably ill-trained and not well brought up. A lazy house wrecker does not wake up early but is rather full of excuses and arguments about why things are not done.

Be a virtuous woman and set aside all forms of inappropriate sleep. Be a virtuous woman and just get up early and cut out the excuses. Get to the job and provide for your household. Gird your loins with strength after a good night's sleep. Make sure that you rise early.

CHAPTER 4

The Evils that Befall
a Sleeper

For the light makes everything visible. This is why it
is said,

"Awake, O sleeper,

 rise up from the dead,

 and Christ will give you light."

                                    Ephesians 5:14 (NLT)

I n this chapter, you will discover what it means to be a sleeper. Decide that you will not be a sleeper by arising to your work, arising to do your work. A sleeper is someone who sleeps too much.

1. **A sleeper is somebody who walks in *evil deeds*.** If you are engulfed in evil deeds, you are a sleeper.

    Take no part in the worthless DEEDS OF EVIL and darkness; instead, expose them.

    It is shameful even to talk about the things that ungodly people do in secret.

    But their evil intentions will be exposed when the light shines on them,

    for the light makes everything visible. This is why it is said,"Awake, O sleeper, rise up from the dead, and Christ will give you light."

    So be careful how you live. Don't live like fools, but like those who are wise.

    Make the most of every opportunity in these evil days.

    Don't act thoughtlessly, but understand what the Lord wants you to do.

    Ephesians 5:11-17 (NLT)

2. **A sleeper is someone who walks in *darkness*.** A person who is a sleeper is walking in darkness. Darkness speaks of deception. Remember that as you deceive people you are also being deceived. Watch out and be careful that you live your life in the light. When you walk in the light you are known and you also know more. When you walk in darkness, you cannot see well and people cannot also see you. In the darkness you are deceiving and you are also being deceived.

Take no part in the worthless DEEDS OF EVIL and darkness; instead, expose them.

It is shameful even to talk about the things that ungodly people do in secret.

But their evil intentions will be exposed when the light shines on them,

for the light makes everything visible. This is why it is said, "AWAKE, O SLEEPER, rise up from the dead, and CHRIST WILL GIVE YOU LIGHT."

Ephesians 5:11-14 (NLT)

3. **A sleeper is someone who operates in *secret.*** Are you a man of secrets? Are you a woman of many secrets? Then you are a sleeper. You need to arise from your sleep. You need to wake out of your secret life of evil deeds and arise out of the dead.

Take no part in the worthless deeds of evil and darkness; instead, expose them.

It is shameful even to talk about THE THINGS THAT UNGODLY PEOPLE DO IN SECRET.

But their evil intentions will be exposed when the light shines on them,

for the light makes everything visible. This is why it is said, "AWAKE, O SLEEPER, RISE UP FROM THE DEAD, and Christ will give you light."

Ephesians 5:11-14 (NLT)

4. **A sleeper is somebody who constantly *falls into temptation* because he is prayerless.** Are you a sleeper? If you are a sleeper then you will fall into many temptations. Peter and the disciples fell into the temptation of betraying the Lord. They fell into that temptation because they were sleepers. Arise out of your sleepy Christian life so that you will be delivered out of multiple temptations. Read the Bible carefully. Those

who sleep, fall into many temptations and are not able to overcome because they do not have enough spiritual strength.

Then cometh Jesus with them unto a place called Gethsemane, and saith unto the disciples, Sit ye here, while I go and pray yonder.

And he took with him Peter and the two sons of Zebedee, and began to be sorrowful and very heavy.

Then saith he unto them, My soul is exceeding sorrowful, even unto death: tarry ye here, and watch with me.

And he went a little further, and fell on his face, and prayed, saying, O my Father, if it be possible, let this cup pass from me: nevertheless not as I will, but as thou wilt.

AND HE COMETH UNTO THE DISCIPLES, AND FINDETH THEM ASLEEP, AND SAITH UNTO PETER, WHAT, COULD YE NOT WATCH WITH ME ONE HOUR?

WATCH AND PRAY, THAT YE ENTER NOT INTO TEMPTATION: THE SPIRIT INDEED IS WILLING, BUT THE FLESH IS WEAK.

Matthew 26:36-41

5. A sleeper is somebody whose behaviour causes the *sheep to be scattered.*

YOUR SHEPHERDS ARE SLEEPING, O king of Assyria; Your officers are lying down. Your people are scattered on the mountains and there is no one to gather them.

Nahum 3:18 (NASB)

When a shepherd is a sleeper the sheep are scattered. It is hard work to be a shepherd. Farming involves hard personal effort and labour. God will bless you when you are a hard-working shepherd who does not sleep too much. Get up and pray for your people. Arise and shine! Would you like to be flying in a plane whose pilot has fallen asleep?

Would you be happy if you were told that the pilot of your plane loves sleeping so much that he has to take several naps throughout the flight, leaving the plane to cruise by itself? I do not think so. You would expect the pilot to be awake throughout the flight whilst you sleep.

CHAPTER 5

How to Wake People Up

For the light makes everything visible. This is why it is said,

"Awake, O sleeper,

rise up from the dead,

and Christ will give you light."

Ephesians 5:14 (NLT)

1. Wake people up by calling them.

And ere the lamp of God went out in the temple of the Lord, where the ark of God was, and SAMUEL WAS LAID DOWN TO SLEEP; THAT THE LORD CALLED SAMUEL: and he answered, Here am I.

1 Samuel 3:3-4

2. Wake people up by making them sing. When people are made to sing in the choir, they wake up spiritually.

Thy dead men shall live, together with my dead body shall they arise. AWAKE AND SING, YE THAT DWELL IN DUST: for thy dew is as the dew of herbs, and the earth shall cast out the dead.

Isaiah 26:19

3. Wake people up by stirring them up. You can stir people up by the gift of God.

Wherefore I put thee in remembrance THAT THOU STIR UP THE GIFT OF GOD, which is in thee by the putting on of my hands.

2 Timothy 1:6

4. Wake people up by provoking them.

And let us consider one another TO PROVOKE UNTO LOVE AND to good works:

Hebrews 10:24

You can provoke people to love and good works by preaching stirring messages to rouse them up in the service of God. Many of my young people are stirred up to serve God because they have been provoked to join the ministry.

5. Wake people up by showing them the right thing to do.

AWAKE TO RIGHTEOUSNESS, and sin not; for some have not the knowledge of God: I speak this to your shame.

1 Corinthians 15:34

You will be surprised that people love to be shown the way of holiness and righteousness. Preaching about the cross of Jesus Christ does not drive people away from God. It draws them to God. People come to church because they want to know God and they want to be holy. People want to be righteous. People want to know how to serve God.

6. Wake people up by making them sober up.

Therefore let us not sleep, as do others; but let us watch and be sober.

1 Thessalonians 5:6

Whatever is influencing you must be cut off so that you are alert, sober and awake in God. You must put away alcohol, otherwise you will soon be declared a sleeper. You must put away any person who is influencing you wrongly. That person is lulling you to sleep. You need to be alert and awake.

7. Wake people up by telling them to arise and go over the nearest river. Tell them to cross the nearest obstacle. Arise into action and cross the rivers that keep you from The Promised Land.

Moses my servant is dead; NOW THEREFORE ARISE, GO OVER THIS JORDAN, thou, and all this people, unto the land which I do give to them, even to the children of Israel.

Joshua 1:2

8.   **Wake people up by telling them to arise and move away from dangers around them.** Many people are unaware of the dangers that they are in. You need to speak to them sharply, strongly and tell them to arise in the name of Jesus.

And being warned of God in a dream that they should not return to Herod, they departed into their own country another way.

And when they were departed, behold, THE ANGEL OF THE LORD APPEARETH TO JOSEPH IN A DREAM, SAYING, ARISE, AND TAKE THE YOUNG CHILD AND HIS MOTHER, AND FLEE INTO EGYPT, and be thou there until I bring thee word: for Herod will seek the young child to destroy him.

Matthew 2:12-13

9.   **Wake people up by telling them to arise and obey God, even if it is controversial.**

I WAS IN THE CITY OF JOPPA PRAYING: AND IN A TRANCE I SAW A VISION, A certain vessel descend, as it had been a great sheet, let down from heaven by four corners; and it came even to me:
Upon the which when I had fastened mine eyes, I considered, and saw fourfooted beasts of the earth, and wild beasts, and creeping things, and fowls of the air.
AND I HEARD A VOICE SAYING UNTO ME, ARISE, PETER; SLAY AND EAT.

Acts 11:5-7

10. **Wake people up by telling them about the danger of the roaring lion.**

Be sober, be vigilant; because your adversary the devil, as a roaring lion, walketh about, seeking whom he may devour:

1 Peter 5:8

Anagkazo

Second Edition

Compelling Power!

DAG HEWARD-MILLS

Parchment House

Unless otherwise stated, all Scripture quotations are taken from the King James Version of the Bible.

ANAGKAZO

Copyright © 1998, 2014 Dag Heward-Mills
1st printing 2014

First Edition published by Parchment House 1998
Published by Lux Verbi.BM (Pty) Ltd. 2008
2nd Printing 2008

Second Edition published by Parchment House 2014
15th Printing 2019

[77]Find out more about Dag Heward-Mills
Healing Jesus Crusade
Write to: evangelist@daghewardmills.org
Website: www.daghewardmills.org
Facebook: Dag Heward-Mills
Twitter: @EvangelistDag

ISBN 978-1-61395-486-7

Contents

1.   Anagkazo, Biazo and Anaideia..1

2.   Why Anagkazo is Important...5

3.   How to Practice Anagkazo 9

4.   How to Practice Anaideia and Biazo 21